P9-COP-946

on the space station

Carron Brown

Illustrated by
Bee Johnson

Kane Miller
A DIVISION OF EDC PUBLISHING

A space station flies
above Earth.

Take a trip in a rocket and zoom far from
our planet to visit the astronauts who
live and work in a space station.

Shine a flashlight behind the page
or hold it up to the light to reveal what
is hidden in and around the space station.
Discover a world of great surprises.

Three astronauts will travel to the space station in a spaceship. They will be in space for many months.

Can you see what the train is pulling?

Creak!

Rattle!

The train is moving a huge, heavy rocket.
The rocket will blast the spaceship into space.

The train takes a few hours to slowly move
the rocket from the building where it was
made to the launchpad.

About three hours before liftoff, the astronauts board the spaceship, which is inside the top part of the rocket.

5...4...3...2...1

Blast off!

What happens as the rocket shoots into the air?

The three long arms holding
the rocket fall away as it
blasts into the air.

It takes only 45 seconds to
reach a speed of more than
1,000 miles per hour.

Roar!

Nine minutes later, the spaceship leaves the rocket, which tumbles back down to Earth.

Where are the astronauts?

Whoosh!

The astronauts are strapped
safely inside the spaceship.
They will continue their
journey to the space station.

The astronauts
are traveling at
a speed of five
miles per second.
That's very fast!

Can you see the
space station?

Zoom!

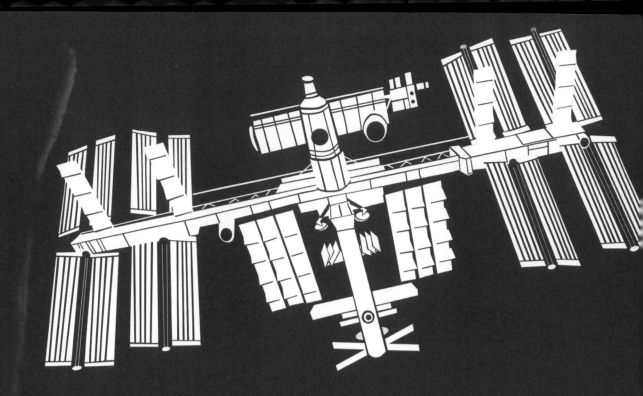

The space station is orbiting (circling around) Earth.

The astronauts have to chase and catch the space station so they can dock.

This can take up to two days!

At last,
the spaceship
joins one of
the four docking
ports on the
space station.

What do the
astronauts
find inside
the space
station?

Hello!

The astronauts open the hatch and meet the crew already on the space station.

The astronauts seem to be floating inside the space station.

What happens when this bag of candy is opened?

CANDY

The candies rise out of the package!
They move slowly through the air.

The candies and the
astronauts look like
they're floating.
This is called
weightlessness.

Whee!

It's time to
get some sleep.
The astronauts tie their
sleeping bags to the station walls.
If they aren't tied to something,
the bags will float around.

Can you see two more astronauts sleeping?

Zzzz.

Some astronauts sleep in small cabins that are the size of a cupboard.

The astronauts can wear eye masks to block out the lights that are always on inside the space station.

Astronauts are busy from the moment they wake up. They have to work, but they need to keep fit, too. They exercise for two hours every day.

Which exercise machine is this astronaut using?

The astronaut is using a
running machine to keep fi
He is strapped in to keep
him from floating away.

Whirr!

Astronauts see 16 sunrises and 16 sunsets as the space station travels around Earth.

They also see the Moon, which is orbiting Earth. It is very far away.

Can you see any cities on Earth?

As the Sun sets, city
lights are turned on.
Hello, people
on Earth!

Zap!

There's also work to do inside the station. Experiments are studied over several months in the station's three science labs.

Can you see what's living in the tank?

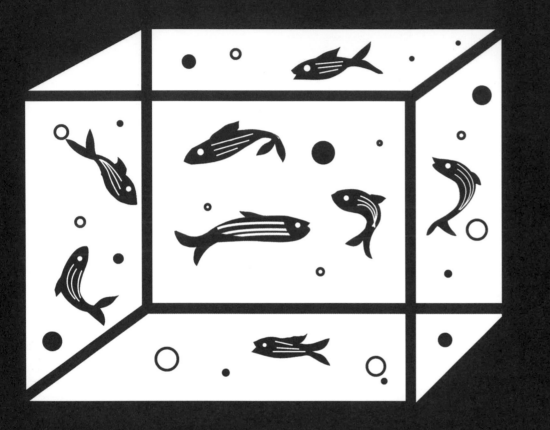

Flick!

Swish!

Zebrafish swim in the tank.
Astronauts study them to
see how they live in space.

One of the astronauts is getting ready to work outside the space station.

There is no air to breathe in space. The astronaut is wearing a space suit that provides air and keeps him safe.

Can you see him inside it?

Zip!

Under his space suit,
the astronaut wears a
thin layer of clothing.

He also has a microphone
and headphones to talk
to the other astronauts.

This astronaut is using controls inside the space station to move a giant robotic arm.

Can you see what's on the end of the arm?

Drrrr!

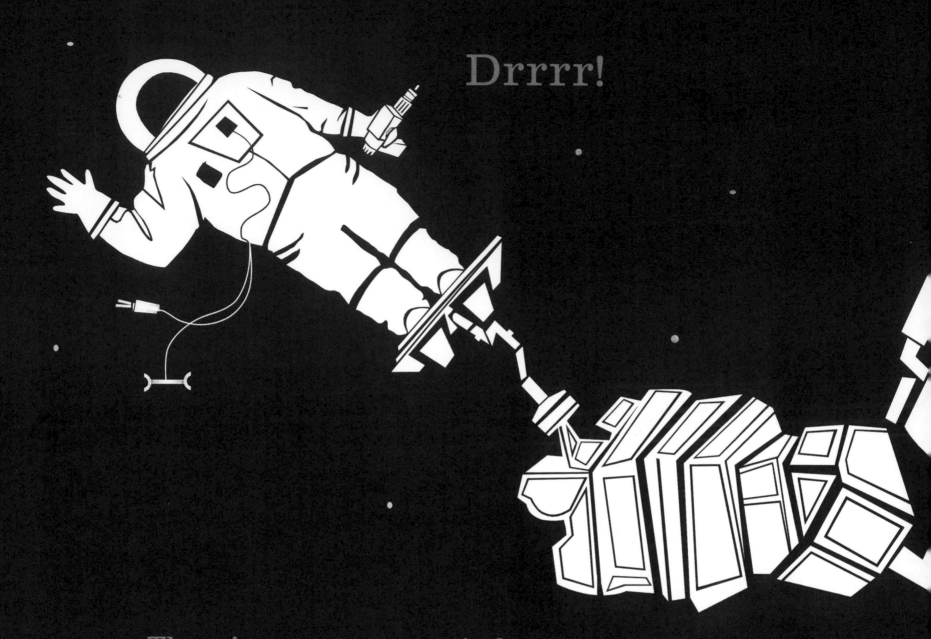

There's an astronaut tied
to the arm. The controls will
take him to a part of the space
station that needs repair.
His tools are tied to his suit to
keep them from floating away.

The astronauts can call home on their computers at any time.

What are the astronauts looking at?

Hello
from Earth!

The astronauts can see their families as they are speaking to them. Their families can see them, too.

The astronauts enjoy a meal together before three of them leave for Earth. The food is in containers so that it will last a long time. Fresh food is a real treat.

Can you see what's inside these containers?

Yum!

There's raspberry yogurt, shrimp cocktail, and chicken soup. There can be hundreds of different foods and drinks to choose from!

After six months, it's time to go home. The astronauts set off in the spaceship and Mission Control talks to them to help them land safely.

Can you see how the spaceship lands?

There's more...

There is a lot of equipment needed for each space station mission!

Launchpad The rocket takes off from a special platform called the launchpad. The rocket is large and heavy, so it must be carried to the launchpad by train.

Spaceship At the top of the rocket is the spaceship. The spaceship brings the astronauts to and from the space station. Inside, it has room for three astronauts, and it also carries food and water to the space station.

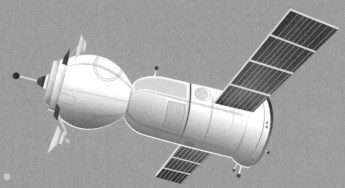

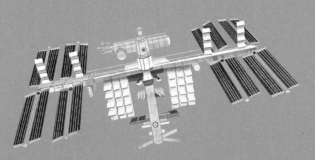

Space station The International Space Station is a big spacecraft that orbits the Earth. It is the biggest object ever flown in space. People can live in it for many months. It has two bathrooms and a gym, and it has been visited by astronauts from 15 different countries. At night, it looks like a bright star, which can be seen from Earth.

Sleeping cabin Each sleeping cabin in the space station is big enough for just one person and has its own sleeping bag.

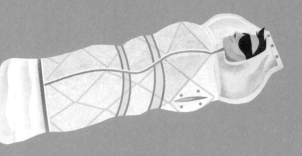

Space suit Astronauts wear special suits which cover them from head to toe so it is safe to go outside the space station. The astronauts carry oxygen in backpacks. This gas is fed into their helmets to help the astronauts breathe. Lights on their helmets help the astronauts to see.

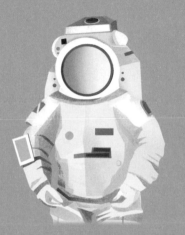

Robotic arm A robotic arm is a little like a crane. Objects or astronauts can be attached to the end of the arm and moved around the outside of the space station to make any repairs that are needed.

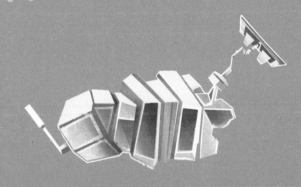

Science lab While they are in the space station, astronauts do science experiments in rooms called labs. These labs contain special equipment to help the astronauts discover more about how humans and animals live in space, and also to see how plants grow.

First American Edition 2016
Kane Miller, A Division of EDC Publishing

Copyright © 2017 Quarto Publishing plc

Published by arrangement with Ivy Kids, an imprint of The Quarto Group.
All rights reserved. No part of this book may be reproduced, transmitted
or stored in an information retrieval system in any form or by any means, graphic,
electronic or mechanical, including photocopying, taping and recording,
without prior written permission from the publisher.

For information contact:
Kane Miller, A Division of EDC Publishing
PO Box 470663
Tulsa, OK 74147-0663
www.kanemiller.com
www.edcpub.com
www.usbornebooksandmore.com

Library of Congress Control Number: 2015938834

Printed in China

ISBN: 978-1-61067-411-9